BANANA HEART

RITA MOOKERJEE

POETRY

stb

STEEL TOE BOOKS
est. 2003

Steel Toe Books
steeltoebooks.com

For special discounted bulk purchases, please contact sales@steeltoebooks.com

BANANA HEART

TABLE OF CONTENTS

THE TROPICS

THE HIGHWAY

THE NECROPOLIS

THE TROPICS

Nocturne with Helium Balloons Lost on the Denver Airport Ceiling

Clustered tightly, the balloons look like baby
fruit bats hiding from everything outside like
the cursed statue of that demonic blue horse:

the true symbol of America, trillion-cut ruby
eyes mocking our pain. American life is about
picking your poison. We accept the reality that

something somewhere someone is going to get you.
Maybe sinkholes, the IRS, carbon monoxide,
the KKK, or even just the wind which might be

what swept all these wild balloons into a peak
of the airport ceiling which is billowy and sloped
like a circus tent, a fitting venue because what is

late capitalism and commerce if not high theater?
I want to go home. I stare at the balloons. Their
loud candy colors are nothing like the milky sunset

we watch from an airport platform lined in fake grass
for dogs to pee on. Honestly, the strips of faux turf
look much nicer than any of the plains right now,

with their poisonous runoff and apologetic yellow
grass. In recent years, Colorado has been catching
fire. You can spot the burnt patch in the shadow

of the Rockies. I watch the coastline turn
to mush while landfills become castles of filth.
It's been years since I felt like I had any connection

to this land which I now see was never mine to claim.
I confess: I have no interest in canyons. The famed
amber waves of grain are tainted and sour. Even

the most majestic mountains slouched and softened
with age. Grey, not purple. Besides, I prefer the sloping
shoulders of my Appalachian chain rich with Douglas

firs and boysenberry bushes. At least for now. When
they're gone, I want to sail away on a convincing breeze
just like one of the lost balloons, pink with optimism.

I always thought the collapse of this empire would be blue
flames and glorious wreckage and bandanas and chanting, but
now that I cut America open, all I really find is hot air.

On Dumb Souvenirs and the Taking Spirit

At security check, island-bound ladies gather.
I recall that the closer I get to the equator, the more
I start to look like everyone else, the more the world
seems old and familiar. Lately, I've noticed how
New York dries my nose and leaves grey skin
around my lips, my mouth shedding itself, my body
peeling away into America. When my gate

changes, I have to go outside. I absorb fine mist,
already dreaming of the island, already a sponge.
I think of American tourists who take saltbleached
seashells from the islands, who tuck mini bottles of rum
into their carry-ons, little totems to rest on office
desks and Pottery Barn nightstands, who visit the craft
park to buy black dolls dressed like schoolchildren
in paper bag brown uniforms. I think of those who
fly into Montego Bay to avoid seeing poor people
on the Kingston streets. I too will take. I carry the taking
spirit on my passport, on my visa. The scholar abroad;
how novel. I think of the president leering on the news,
blaming drugs on Jamaica, calling Haiti a shithole.
I want to wipe my America off.

I am destined to take, this is certain, but I will myself
into something soft and pliant to the world around me
cosmic or not. I transform myself into a sponge: ready
to give just as much as I take.

Happy Hour in the Wetlands

Why isn't there a word for plants that eat meat /
carnivorous doesn't begin to describe the subversion
that is the sundew / splayed like a ten-finger hand dotted
with nectar / patient nightmare / ready to turn nature
on its head / I'm bored of lions and gazelles / that hunt
is so predictable and though everyone remembers the
venus flytrap / there's the sundew the waterwheel the
byblis the pitcher plant / people find them sinister / what
with their meat-eating and all / I guess I can relate / to
their pragmatism / rooted in bland soil trying to make
things more interesting / playing tricks on all the flies /
here comes one now / to the sundew at peak posture /
diamond spheres humming sticky seduction / red veins
/ a riddle a clue / and the flyboy makes mistake number
one / getting a closer look / oh you've done it now
flyboy / watch how he writhes fibers binding / getting
glued to himself / the sundew exhales / starts to undulate
like a belly dancer / as our fly panics / shifting spineless /
his last free leg in arabesque / and there might as well be
a cocktail straw in his back / happy hour in the wetlands
/ later sundew sated untendrils in the sun as a fluorescent
scroll wouldn't you like to give me a try.

Lost Girl Considers Her Lack of Heirlooms

All I ever wanted was an old keepsake.
Everyone seems to have them but me:
a pen knife, brass kettle, grandmother's pearls.
I met her once, and the only thing my grandmother ever
gave me was a wet kiss and a book:
the diary of anne frank, which I'd read already.

I sound entitled. I would love to get over it already
but mental illness is as close as I get to keepsake
territory which is disappointing. Not like I hated the book.
I wish my grandmother should have shared with me
stories that I had never read before: tales for whenever
I feel scared: to hold in my palms like warm pearls

meant to weigh me down for sleep, pearls
that are never cool to the touch because someone was already
holding them before me.   But really, if I ever
mix too much wine and klonopin, know that I left a keepsake
atop every shelf in my place. Just shards of me
that you can divide amongst yourselves. The book-

shelves are where I lived, and any book
that lived with me stayed pristine like pearls
beaming from lucky oyster shells. One thing about me:
I refuse to write in books. Hello? There is already
a story here. No need for the unwanted keepsake
of someone else's words. If there was ever

an opposite to the heirloom, that'd be a curse. Ever
the optimist, I know. I'm just saying that the book
dadi gave me would have been more like a keepsake
if it was super old with pages thinning so that light pearls
here and there lighting the words aflame. I already
know that this will remain a fantasy for me,

the daydreamer, little old disappointed, diasporic me.
All alone in America   so whenever
I get sentimental, I tell the mirror to perk up already.
shake it off, bitch. Self-pity is basic. I book
a hair appointment. I dust my cheeks in gold and glue pearls
to my temples. Forget an old necklace, I'll be my own keepsake

just like anne's lilac teacup, a keepsake already
better guarded than me, someone who never learns and pearls
wisdom for pennies. Books are doomed to burn;
put mine in the fire for me.

Banana Heart

While tending the garden, Christina spots something
strange. I hate Florida but I'll go anywhere for girlfriends

and good tacos, and thankfully, her pocket hometown doesn't
give me greasy wedgie sandal tan vibes or buy-one-get-one

coladas that taste like lotion and wax. In her Florida, my hair
reddens and I leave piles of half-shells in my wake, forever lusting

after oyster juice, and once I saw a leatherback weaving through
dark dunes, that cretaceous queen unphased by mortal gawkers,

weary from hours of tilling sand into cradles. Christina's Florida
cups the turtle in foam then shimmies its shoulders and flicks

moonbeams at skinny dippers. On the night before her wedding,
she was dreaming of a heat-dappled canopy that would be hers.

Now she sleeps under top-heavy, smooth-trunk trees and strange
blooms in a little temple with lemon-topped pillars and idols

wreathed in orange with open mouths breathing wet and hot
to save energy for guttural chanting in the night: those ancient prayers

for Christina and her mother who chanted on holy days in Leyte
before tending chicken coops on the farm. She still chants on Sundays,

though it is Tuesday in the tallest fronds when Christina looks in
the center of a baby banana cluster and finds a decadent object neither

symmetrical nor round, but tear-shaped and unyielding. She cuts down
the bunch and sap comes in rivulets down her arm, so much more than

sugar. I dream of the banana heart and the rest of the fruits Christina
grows in the temple garden where you can't tell if you're in Cocoa Beach

or the Visayas and I may never grow a banana heart of my own, so I remind her to document blossoms that announce fruits and spend lots of time in the trees. The bananas are the nest, and she the egg.

Soliloquy With Colonizer Logic

Marie Antoinette? Simone de Beauvoir?
Coco Chanel? If I saw any of them in my kitchen,
I would laugh like step aside, Gabbie, you never
could sauté worth a damn. Because the kitchen is
my arena of choice, the stage of postcolonial revenge,
because what good is the America Dream if you can't
enact a little vengeance, snatch the crown, and colonize
the colonizers here and there? What fun is being middle
class if you can't whip out your organic beet powder
and your stand mixer and your commodity fetish and say
hey, ça va, you French fucks? I made your insane cookies
that you have to beat then coddle then pipe and pray over
while they bake as you hope for those perfect footed ridges
and like your Chantilly lace and wine classification, this is
very complicated. But goddamn it, I made it. I solved it,
I'm as good as French and really that is American: doing
the absolute most no matter how high or how low the stakes;
did you know? I always whip my meringue by hand.

I Cancel Your Plane Tickets

since you won't be coming to the island the way we've
been planning for months, it's a pretty ideal time to break

the news to me. After weeks of fighting, I pull up pictures
of the bamboo hut on the water that we chose, though we

knew that a single ceiling fan would do little to cool us
after fucking and drinking. After all, neither you nor I

would be caught dead in some sterile all-inclusive joint or
a cheesy cruise ship like the one where those people sat

stranded off the California coast, now cursed with a fortnight
in airport quarantine. Serve them right, I half-joked. All they

do is steal shells and jars of sand and underpay the locals. I
joke too much which is part of why you're ending things.

I pictured taking you to get coconut water on the roadside
where they cut the coarse shells to make spoons for scooping

out the white jelly. I imagined taking our pick of fishermen
wins to fry and eat somewhere nearby with callaloo and

plantains. All of this could have been if not for my temper,
You know, we could have fled to the hut in Oracabessa which is

not far from Kingston, though I was hesitant to travel. I didn't
want our week together wasted on a bus because I never seem

to take trips that feel like vacation. There is usually an odd
smell, an allergic reaction, a hangover; something to wedge

itself between rest and me. Of course, this would have been
your vacation, not mine. Kingston is just where I work despite

days spent drinking soursop on the veranda, dancing on Water
Lane against the juicy backdrops of street murals fresh on old

stone. I wanted to take you up Stony Hill where the roads have
no guard rails and bromeliads peer from their tree trunk anchors.

Catalpa pods litter the way to the top where you can see all of
Kingston and its crown of mountains. You love to hike and walk,

but I don't think I could make it both ways on foot. I'd call
a friend to drive us up so you could get a view that is nothing like

your flat Iowa city. In secret I wished that you would get stranded
here, barred from re-entering the U.S. Your mother would have been

inconsolable while you stressed about your research, antsy
without your lasers and lab. But I would have been beyond content.

You would have napped while I laughed at the stock market, smoking
and writing at length until blackbirds and waxbills screamed you awake.

Don't Trifle With Baboon Queens

In my hate mail, I spot the words you fucking baboon which
fascinates me. What a specific primate to name. I guess monkey

wasn't enough or maybe they couldn't tell if I was black brown yellow
red enough to earn a more tried and true slur. I confuse them which

only makes them angrier. But that anger is nothing compared to female
baboons who roll up in packs of 50 and more. There is nothing more

important to them than the matriline and Ancient Egyptians called them
sacred which is fitting for any such society, unyielding and divine.

In the Atlas Mountains, male baboons battle for the approval of the ladies
and they are only invited to stay if they act right. When they don't

the ladies pull up and give a warning—stretching their faces long to
show off rows of serrated teeth. If a quick threat doesn't work, they

knuckle up darting from cliff to cliff to deliver a wallop followed by
a vampiric lunge for the jugular. One young dude gets pinned down

against the black shale. He shrieks after, maybe from the bite or maybe
just out of shame. Either way, this is a good lesson and he really should

shriek. Because the truth is that he might be the same as them and maybe
even kin, but one hungry evening, he might get cannibalized all the same.

While Cooking Salmon Sous Vide, I Consider the Futility of Courtship

In one smooth motion, I seal the filet
inside a plastic womb. The safest place.
I assume that this fish was male, but it's
hard to say. Males have heavy jaws, big heads.
In mating season, fish heads swell. Protrude.
While males bulk up and redden, the females
turn green. I can't make this up.
I perform a funeral in a deep,
shiny pot. Gently, I offer the fish
to the water, its rosy flesh bathed in
honey and miso, banded like a tree
stump. I try to read between the white lines;
the moral is lost in the marinade.
Segments of flesh never kiss and tell.

Shrine

In the market, Rayanne arranges
breadfruit and guava on her stand.
She frames them with squat pumpkins
and green hooks of plantain. She
leans against her stool to stretch her
legs, finished with curation. She ties
up her braids and calls over to Cecile
selling vegetables two stands over.

Like many market women, Rayanne
says hands off the goods, but she makes
exceptions to this rule for the college
kids, the ones far from their homes in
Saint Lucia and Barbados. Rayanne
learns their names, asks about their studies.
She brings them over to touch the squash
and the June plums. In return, they tell her
the fruit words they use back home:
christophine, pomme-settiere. She laughs.

All of this happens far downtown,
around the corner from stray dogs with
short coats and long tongues. All of this
happens near the labyrinth of old crates
built by ghosts and drifters who are dead
asleep on the pavement. But this is

all that is left in the frame of a NatGeo
photo for an article about black poverty,
crime, death. Probably. Let them say
death, danger, dirt, rot. The longer they
think this, the longer Rayanne, the fresh
fruits, this place can stay sacred.

Elegy in August Town

The taxi man asks how I am coping with the recent incidents
on Hermitage Road. When I ask what happened he says violence

and before he tells me about the young man, I already know exactly
what happened. He says violence and the word bursts from its skin,

a word that leaves more words in its wake, almost always the same:
recent string of   teenage   investigation   pavement   unknown.

Back home, when the news says BREAKING, I inhale and wait
for the picture, which is usually a school photo. People tend to keep

those on hand. Here in Kingston, the boy's aunt doesn't have one.
It is her face in the paper instead, caught mid-speech with a clenched

hand and jaw to match. She is saying enough because 13 years ago,
her son was shot, her daughter, now her nephew who was making

his way back from the market with yams, okra, and Scotch bonnets, his
Tuesday ritual. The paper reads DEATH STALKS AUGUST TOWN.

I know that this plague is not unique to the island. Against my will,
I have lost count of the dead back home. I have forgotten too many

of the names belonging to black bodies left too long on asphalt, many
gone before they grew facial hair or learned to drive. This too is an act

of violence of which I am guilty. The taxi man's name is Rondell. He
mistakes me for an islander—Guyanese or Trini. He sighs, what has

happened to us? He doesn't know that I'm just an import. Just a brown
Yankee nerd in her tortoiseshell glasses who hoped that things would

be different here, that black boys could jog home after rugby, bend to
knot their shoelaces, grab Ting from the gas station and make it back

from the market. When I look at the paper, at the aunt's fury, I know that black boys in a black country are not safe in the way I imagined.

As Rondell turns onto the college campus, a student bolts onto the road to jaywalk. In an instant, Rondell stops. He lets the student cross.

With a guilty smile the young man waves in gratitude. He looks like a first year, maybe the same age as the boy who was killed. Rondell waves back, calls from the window, muss protect the next generation.

On the Violence of Tanzanite
    Liguanea, Kingston

It's Thursday when tourists find their way into the plaza.
They want mini bongs and big tees in yellow,
red, and black. Some ladies eye the rings, mostly
dated and overdone except for a couple pieces
with odd violet stones. Picture the one from the Titanic,
the necklace the old woman drops into the water. I hate
that movie. I feel no love for the deadly rich, richly dead
or those penciled breasts atop the floating door.

What is it with white people on ships making bad decisions?
Like how about the assholes who ignored the CDC
two weeks ago, said screw the virus! and got on the Pacific
Princess anyway. They all live in vacation purgatory now,
stranded right outside Cali with a clear view of home
and no path in sight. Was it worth it? To eat frozen food
on a boat? Next to me a lady coos over a pearl cluster,
nodules fat like salmon roe. She thumbs a slim pendant.
Mistakes it for amethyst. But I know the true stone well.

I'm tipsy on Appleton rocks at the bar, so I imagine peeking over
my shades to say *What if I told you that those elegant inky stones*
come from a dusty mouth where strapped guards pace back
and forth scanning the water and the horizon for little kids
or thieves bold enough to climb to the mine after sunset?
Worse yet to see the tanzanite mining by day. Rocks hewn
and pried apart by greying fingers already shaking at the start
of a 20-hour shift because no, these beauties aren't from this island
or any island at all. These rocks were trafficked here by white
people on ships, sailed across two oceans, unpacked in crates.
To be clear, every commodity comes with conflict. There is no
beauty that humans can fathom without spilling some blood.

THE HIGHWAY

Anhedonia, Let's Get Lost
after Carrie McGath

No matter how basic, there is always something satisfying about a
freshly unwrapped bar of soap waiting in a clean shower even in a
Spartan presentation: perched on a faucet head like a milky talisman.
No matter what, we don't skip the skincare routine, hence the motel.
The bathroom tiles are lime and pink. There's something I didn't tell
you. No matter how hard I try, I can't get into kitsch. I love flamingos
and red arrows and dancing teeth and neon horses in theory, but up
close they make me queasy. They remind me how boring real life is. At
the bar, I watch you shoot tequila and smoke. I briefly consider stealing
your beret and putting in under my pillow to see who would show up.
Unlike most, I'm not a betting woman, but my money would be on
Mae West. Maybe she would look at us in our long black dresses and
say something charming about whose funeral. Maybe she would grant
me a wish; it's nice to be on the receiving end.

Litany of Bad Habits, Millennial Edition

Still midnight snacking. Still drinking &
overcommitting & overspending & oversleeping.
Still biting the crust off tubes of superglue
instead of cutting the tip off with a knife.
Still picking fights with strangers online.
Still running with scissors. Still cursing.
Still letting my glasses slide down my nose.
Still hot-tempered. Still largely unknown.
Still figuring out my eyebrows. Still pulling
tights up to my bra though the waistband pinches.
Still calling women I hate a bunch of looking ass
bitches. Still joking about work life balance
instead of leaving for a job that might love me back.
Still picking scabs once the wounds lie flat.
Still shopping for a god & blaming stars for problems.
Still using illicit drugs. Still dreaming of the heiress
in a turquoise necklace. Still not speaking to her
& probably never will simply out of spite.
Still sleeping in my makeup. Still restless.
Still can't tell if there's a fruit fly infestation
or if this time around, I just died in the night.

Ode to Bathroom Mirror Altars I've Built for Myself

I'm moving back east to a basement studio that
barely holds my furniture, but you know what?
It's got a closet just for my makeup. The bathroom
lighting is exquisite. I know. It's hardly an upgrade,
but the planet is on fire. I'd rather stay inside
loving myself at the medicine cabinet, glowing
tiers of glass potions and indulgences and there
I am: the patron saint of queer brown femmes
in my cold sepulcher painting myself to life so I
can stomp into the day and silently tell the world
not to fuck with me. My eyebrows are Disney villain
pointy for a reason. I can do them on the train, forget
a mirror. My hands are steady like a bass line from
all my practice in foggy compacts and bumpy bus

rides. Listen, I'm downsizing. I leave my small vanity
near the alleyway its surface scuffed by bobby pins
and blunts rolled in pink paper, from acrylic towers
of mocha lipsticks less than half a shade apart.
I'll miss my vanity, but I don't need it. No one
can tell if you get ready curved over a single stall
sink with a spiderweb mirror or if you beat your
face beatified in ring light flanked by cherry
perfect studio bulbs sitting in a wingback chair
in tufted blush velvet. This is about the finished
product: big reveals with feather fans shimmying.
I silently thank my vanity for its service, but

it was never made for a gay millennial femme.
A woman says to me you'll outgrow all of that but
I know the truth: to me, every painted lashline is
a landscape. Every brushstroke on my face is
an ancient ritual in repetition, so the next time
I'm flush with cash, I'm buying booze, lights, plus
more lipstick. I'm going out screaming in full glam.

In Hell, I Forget About Busking, Smut, and Stares

ANALOG a shaved head kisses my ass
THAT'S WHAT I'M TALKING BOUT.
I'm shocked by the flood of his voice
brassy like an accordion in the night.
Under a glassy overlay, the bar boasts
saucy pin-ups and seedy dime store
titles too silly to be relics from the past.
One reads LEATHER GIRL: SHE HAD THE FACE
OF AN ANGEL, THE BODY OF THE DEVIL,
AND THE PASSION OF A LESBIAN. I snicker
and a couple turns to look at me, transfixed
though not by my face, though I might still
look good. Even in hell, people are mystified
when they see a woman with a pen and a notebook.

All Nests Begin in the Body

I burned too much frankincense which made all my cobwebs
turn black and heavy enough to drape across your hands. In

doing so I ruined the wares of the black lace weaver whose
creations come mother of pearling from the ceiling. She

is a reminder that someone is always watching, a reminder
to behave myself like the metal springs in my arm that stop

my period—maybe forever—and I kind of miss it if only
for its opaque display, the sheer force of spilling my guts. Once

in a while, it is nice to see what I am made of, no matter how
viscous and dark but not dark like the singed resin in my nails.

Instead a wet color that I can only find inside me, a place I am
often unwilling to go unlike the weaver queen who pulses out

honeyed enzyme calling the hatchlings to her softest parts
calling them to the skeleton key in her abdomen. Unlike me

she is the most capable host and knows exactly what she is made
of saying come here, baby, you don't have to be hungry anymore.

Elegy for Fakir Musafar, the Father of Modern Body Piercing

Ronald Loomis falls into a dream
on a South Dakota reservation in 1942 and in that dream

he learns that the body can be changed
in the practice of cave jungle desert dwellers

whose spears and scalpels were divine instruments.
When he wakes up he takes to his own tissue:

barbell animating steel ring tickling, experiments of flesh
for the modern age. The theft of names is a grave sin

but in these years of dreaming and bleeding this man
is a white body who leaves the country to study

and comes back not with trophies only purpose. He
becomes more than a man with a penchant for sticks

and arrows or exposed breasts and lip disks. I don't
know how a man becomes a shaman an ascetic a fakir

and I still fear curious white men who are good
with needles but with each puncture Ronald Loomis

leaked out onto the ground across Lakota land into the soil
of all the world's bloodied people until no Ronald Loomis

was left for this world only a body willing to stretch
and ache and twirl in suspension savage hooks through

pectoral muscles; a bouquet of skewers across his spine
sun dancing above crowds in ecstasy a father reminding

children that there is power in ornament that pain is cyclical
that the body is honeycomb: a series of sockets to be fitted with gems.

A Snake Heart Can Slide Up and Down the Length of Its Body
a golden shovel *after Aimee Nezhukumatathil*

Perhaps this is why I often look at ease. My snake-
skin picks up on any given vibe then tells my heart
where to go.   In this way, I can

always work a room. It is not possible to slide
under my skin. I have no under. I am built up
of earthen lace   part of an infinite body.

My heart bounces through rings of bone, down
my pronged ribs and back up the brief length of
me   like the top   of a carnival game its

bulb screaming then gone.   As a snake, my body
is always ready. It is not possible to stab my heart ;
                    that thing is always on the move.

Magnolia Striptease

Every year I catch that muted perfume but find
the blossoms too late the blush petals already tipped

with brown exhausted from their brush with fame
their spent days of notoriety littering the campus

in slivers of rose and cream like discarded satin slippers
or nipple pasties peeled from the softest peaks of breast.

Someday I will start early and catch them at their fullest, in their
most labial, obscene, and decadent state and though I love bees

they do not interrupt me under the magnolia with her crown of beetles
and so I get a private dance in a bowing maze of strength and softness.

To think that this tree persisted for 50 million years and now
owes a debt to beetles, not bees for its survival. To think that

a body could weather this world for that long and leave me with
nothing but a striptease.

Love Song for the First Dyke Bartender

This was 1925, can you imagine the disappointed faces
so many downturned mustaches? Before the arch and down

MacDougal, that's where Eve Adam's Tearoom used to stand
with its peanut shelled floor, tidy square tables, tea lights

and the sign that read   men permitted but not welcome
painted by Eve herself: shoulders square and both elbows

up carving out her space with a paring knife and really not
giving a fuck about anyone's feelings, Eve kept men on

their toes, sweating them as she skewered olives. Those men
who always stared as if trying to place her, this odd tall broad

who came from Poland as Eva Kotchever. But she dreamt
of a smokey lounge full of lipstick and gloves and had to make

it real and so she transformed because all good queers have
a proper drag name and why not Eve Adams, named for those

original sinners, that face, those leaves, that cage which
held the rib, femme masc mixing that was Eve, shaking things

up with ice cubes in a steel mixer: a powerful weapon in its
own right pouring sapphic elixirs and tonics that smelled

like anise and cumin. But dear Eve, you didn't stay for long.
I wonder if your mouth went dry when the Nazis surged into

Paris, what you wished you drank last before they took you.
Eve, I wish I was there for last call. I'd order a whiskey ginger

and help you wipe down the stools before you locked the doors.
Eve, I would ask to walk you home to that fourth-floor walkup.
Eve, this world was never ready. Even New York couldn't take you.

Self-Portrait as Saint Rita of Cascia Covered in Bees, 1381

i. If you make friends with fear, you'll never be lonely.
And who can feel lonely in a beaded cloak? Oblong yellow
shards humming a bhajan or a warning or a hymn. Sometimes
the bees are a collar locking me in place. Sometimes they make
a halo. Other times they form a veil shielding me from outsiders
who always want and ask and take and take. Be brave, they say.

ii. The swarm is as uncanny as the earthquake that shook Rocco
Porena: an announcement of my birth. Like a fist over my chest
the bees are my seal of sanctity both soothing and lurid. They
always find their way to me when the sun is high and the hollyhocks
are fat. The bees never hurt me. I am known to them like I am known
to the roses at my shine which keep their cold thorns to themselves.

iii. In winter, I dream of the smells of the hive: pollen sharp
in my nose like a pop of static electricity. Be brave. Just wait.
Because every time a mystic is born, a mountain breaks itself
open and ecstatic earth pours forward in sacrifice. As the patron
saint of impossible causes, you get used to eruptions and lots
of noise which is why I never mind all these boys in my hair.

v. I once tried to count them: the threads of my murmuring
robe. I tried to train them, contain them, tell them what to do.
I wanted to hold them in place in a tight fist over my chest.
But now I know that the purpose of the bees is to keep me
listening. Bring me your greatest shame, unprocessed rage.
Be brave. Surrender your secrets to the hum.

Self-Portrait As Samus Aran, 1986

because who else can shoot sharp and pussy pop
in an orange armored suit of power? Don't answer.
It's just me. See, I'm a Virgo and my way is harder
better faster stronger than yours. I've been out here
for decades bounty hunting solo intergalactic style.
My ship is paid for in gold, my gold, and the boots
are bespoke. I'm not trying to fit in. Human DNA be
damned. This was never a game to me and mortality
is boring. I'm trying to cop some bags and maybe a little
vengeance while I'm at it because people never cease to
underestimate me. They are uneasy around girls whose
faces you can't quite make out under a mask. You know
we are trouble. Still you doubt us all the same. If you turn
away for a minute, you won't even see me charge my
morph ball and I don't waste my power. This shit is
sacred and you made it easy so I drop down into a split
and sweep you clean off your feet. Bet you didn't see
that coming. Bet you thought I was a cute little trick
playing dress up coming over to ask you to buy me
a drink. Instead I drag your sorry ass out to hog-tie
and trade for coins. I'm the original cyborg woman
and there are biomechanics between my legs more
precious and intricate than a Fabergé egg. Humans,
pick up your jaws and keep it pushing. Maybe learn
a lesson here: the next time you see me coming, run.

Self-Portrait as the Birthing Statue in Men (2022)

like red apples and missionary on white sheets
your purity culture is boring like your jokes.
like the drone of cicadas. you jerk yourself off
and pretend no one can see you lying on your back
spilling into your mouth, swallowing yourself over
and over. I see all of your indignities, your filth. go on
hit me with your car like you promised you would. everyone
loves a martyr, and I am already pretty exalted for a brown
girl from nowhere who couldn't be bothered with mortality
and moved to new york at the start of the aughts like every
other middle class queer. keep your pastorals, those bucolic
wet dreams. gods don't live in the fields. when it comes
to the divine, fake it til you make it. and you're the last person
who could ever spot a fake. you can't touch me, you don't
scare me, I am the necropolis. I am an emperor swan.
I am a flaming citadel. I am my own congregation.

Men

are the sort of people who
chisel butter from its block
and with a short, blunt knife
pummel it back and forth
across a bready path until
only its stain is left. It never
occurs to them to cut off
a clean square and heat it for
a moment, that butter melts
simply asking to be poured.

THE NECROPOLIS

Kyrielle with the Crown Jewels

I run my brush through my hair like it is all gold thread
like the embroidery dancing on my mom's shalwar.
I covet all things made by hands that are brown.
Give back the jewels you stole for your crown.

I wear my gold, sapphires, and pearls to bed
just in case your avarice continues to spread.
From England, the relics call to me at sundown.
Give back the jewels you stole for your crown.

You heard the Koor-i-Noor's call and traveled so far
for the massive diamond sifted from alluvial ground.
But with all of your looting, you renewed a curse so
give back the jewels you stole for your crown.

The diamonds belong to India, not to your dead.
Our gods planted them: white, yellow, poppy red.
For the sake of your greed, how many Indians bled?
Repent. Give back the jewels you stole for your crown.

Crystal Fisticuffs for Messy Mystics Who Like Rings

I've never left the house without jewelry, without talismans
from my mom, pearls for my name, but lately, I want to add
brass knuckles to the rotation. Though they're kind of plain plus
I doubt there is a set out there to fit my hands. These size 4 fingers
drip in gold and flip the bird but these days, I'm looking to make
a statement and leave an impression. Do you follow me? Because
if I'm gonna swing on somebody, how about something with a little
more bite and next level shine? Gimme that Sailor Moon slap of
sparkle with woodshop dyke practicality. Bespoke, in house-only.
No mass production because this power, this fight is sacred. What
if I could thread my fingers through a crystal ball like here, I hold
your future in the palm of my hand and so sorry to spill the secrets
of the universe but your journey ends here? That's heavy, I know but
spiritually, I can't keep it real without getting messy. And lately, there
are too many Sabrina-wannabe white girls watching too much
American Horror Story, playing too much tarot as if that shit is more
than a game so if you're gonna read something read this: we are at war
and your stolen sage bundles are not helping. You try to keep it earthy
with all those salt lamps and rose quartz, all that Wiccan white supremacy
mined by brown hands for pennies. You don't know the occult, you're
just riding the dick of manifest destiny, so here I come again, the oracle
of bad news for you, boo. Because most of your crystals are plain old glass,
sometimes plastic so the only gleams of truth you get come from sunlight
dancing off Made in China stickers that you didn't think to peel from
the base. These are no allies of mine, so I wanna grab a bunch of queers,
head into the mountains, and dig together for a ridge of amethyst points
that we cut finger holes through but keep jagged and unwashed so that long
after any fight, our enemies will sting pulling muddied slivers from skin.
Even months later, they'll glimpse a shard of something barely violet
inside a callous, a blessed token from us messy mystics who told you:
we are beautiful but from the center of our majik, venom seethes.

Voicemail for Emily Dickinson
after Taylor Byas

Hey, girl. I was at your old house just now.
They're trying to do you dirty. Did you know
they turned that place into a museum?
They even made a replica of that old white
housecoat and stuck it on a mannequin in
your bedroom near your desk like a headless maid
waiting for you to go downstairs so she can snoop
through your shit. Speaking of which, the docent is
uncomfortable talking about your letters.
She says you and old girl used to sleep in the same bed
because it was cold outside, that many Victorian ladies
would have done the same, that it was normal. At least
we can agree on that part. She keeps bringing up the fact
that you didn't have kids like it's confusing, as though
there is something mysterious about wanting peace, quiet,
and endless hours for poetry and repotting plants.
The docent says it doesn't matter who you loved,
that you've only left us with questions. She has it all wrong.
I was at your grave just now. Girl, I shouted your lines
wondering how they can ignore what you told us all along.
But you know what? Plenty of us were listening. Still are.
And I know by all the seashells and rainbow at the base
of your headstone. But listen. I'm nobody, and I'm not
trying to stress you out. By the way, a couple blocks up,
someone planted rows of pink snapdragons. If you
squeeze them gently they open up and grin with rows
of bright yellow teeth. I'll bring you some next time I'm
around. I think you'd like the snapdragons. To hell with the rest.

To Protect Your Children, You Need a Drawer of Hair and Teeth

My mom is a hoarder but not in the popular
sense with dolls and newspapers and putrid
bodies under fallen bookshelves who no one
thought of until the smell kicked in. She is just
too attached to the world. She cannot part
with greeting cards, pacifiers, pastel board
games and wooden souvenirs whose origin
stories tend to change when I ask about them.

There is a drawer in a filing cabinet
where my mom keeps teeth and hair
in envelopes: my sisters canines, the rat
tail my brother sported one summer. It
was in fashion at the time. The envelopes
are labeled with only our names as if we
ourselves lie tucked behind manilla folders.

I think of how the mambos tell people
to bury their hair in the ground so that no
one can take your tresses and ball them
into tufts for ill will. In in this way, my
mom's drawer is fierce protection. It sits
locked in a room within a room within
a room, the key hidden even I don't know where.

Half Ode to the Rope Swing I Never Climbed

There is a length of old rope tied to an elm on the bank of Fishing
Creek that I used to pass on drives with my family. Plenty of kids
jumped from it, but I was never invited to go to Fishing Creek or the
dollop of earth in the middle nicknamed The Beach. Even if I had been
invited, I would not have gone. I knew from science camp how thick
that water was with crayfish, tadpoles, and countless larvae like cyborgs
in their brown armor, antennae, and needling legs. Even if I had been
invited, I would not have jumped. The only brown kid on the bank, too
worried about a graceless descent into the mud, chalky feet calloused
from ballet, arms crossed to protect breasts that took too long to arrive.
Though I never tried the swing, I admired that someone with a ladder
and great care knotted it thrice at the base to support your feet as you
swung. I picture myself there, greening rope in hand. I am fragile like
the mayfly hatchling with no love for stagnant pools. I look to the sun
who knows when it matters, I will choose flight.

Pink Ladies' Smoke Session

Emily brought the weed. Emily also knew how to sculpt
a pipe with a pencil and some rolled tinfoil. What was it
with the dancers and gymnasts? Why did we always
have the drugs while you and the soccer girls gave each
other French braids and never stayed up late? At least
you brought a lighter. When I last saw you, you had
taken up smoking cigarettes. I found that ironic.
I shudder now thinking of what that makeshift bowl
did to our brains, what burning aluminum looks like
as it travels inside a teenage girl. We went into your
first car to smoke, a red Geo Prizm. I picked cat hair
off your shirt while you sprinkled green debris into
the foil. I don't even think we packed a second. We
didn't need to. The glass got foggy as we shotgunned
smoke back and forth, Emily, then you, then me. I see
now that this is the first time you kissed me. I don't know
who you were performing for, but I am sure it was
a performance for you. We slunk inside, wafted
mango body spray, and curled up to watch 16 Candles
together. I tried not to think of the burning foil, of how
our lip balms tasted mixed together. Really, we could
have used an apple. I think you have some pink ladies
upstairs. I said at one point. Neither of you responded.

Abecedarian for a Sale on Cremation

A flier for funerary services appears in my parents' mail-
box.   There's a life insurance policy on the side
crammed in like a bad appetizer special.   Walking
down Lincoln Way   I see a sale for cremation.
Every hair on my arm stands up.   It's buy one get one
free, I kid you not.   And this is what it has come to:
giddy capitalists chomping at the bit, ready to brand our
hell and sell it to us   like we're the lucky ones.
I wonder if they ever lump the bodies together. Do they
just double-stuff the incinerator for the married couples
knowing they can make them spoon   without it being
lurid or in generally poor taste;   less gauche and
more whimsical like two ashen Pompeii lovers knotted
neatly and shielding one another from a blast of doom.
Only the lucky die by volcanic eruption.   There is no
planning or preparation   no tearful days
quietly spent thumbing paperwork, ignoring the phone.
Rifling through photo albums with mouthfuls of dread
sickening and powdery like chalk.   I do not want
to brace myself for my parents' deaths though I have an
underlying suspicion they'll   outlive me with all their
vegetables and constant exercise which is probably
why I can't picture them dead or even dying.   They're
xenolithic fragments that withstand wind and time   so
yes, we are laughing at the death coupon flier. My mom
zests a lemon and cackles   hurry up, time to die.

On Having a Loud-Ass Mouth

As a child, I listened to chickadees and thought,
Enough. You've made your point.
That was before I realized their intentions, their genius,
the audacity of being shrill in the morning calm
first in trills then staccato to herald your rage and go barreling
into the day, to make everyone unsure whether you are thrilled or furious,
                              and I have always been both.

It's bad form to say the word   shrill
when you're talking about women and women's voices
and women's vices, but it's the place where my speeches live
every principled stance, the rickety soapbox ravings
that my friends pretend are both new   and warranted.
In kindergarten, I was told to stop writing in all capital letters
and to never use pen, but I wanted to match my tone,
the serial heckler, a manic maenad shrieking in the drunken background,
the girl who still yells boo and I am forever shouting on high
in an accent, which, like me, cannot be placed.
Sometimes I'm a scholar in sardonic default,
an irate jaywalker, a loud femme at the bar asking for top shelf.

There are women I've known forever
their voices are deeper than I recall.
They all took to smoking cigarettes,
the vice that wouldn't love me back,
and now they all sound like good espresso
and residual eyeliner. It's the rasp, the countershrill,
and sometimes I think I have it, but mostly
it's mucus after a bad cold and for all my screeching
and gritted teeth and belabored points, somewhere,
someone is reading this message and missing my voice
because if nothing else, I know damn well how to leave
an impression. No one hears me and feels neutral.
My mom called me her howler monkey,
an infant orator screeching from a crib
hands through the bars, demanding an audience.

Elegy with Threats, Gifts, and Dead Mice

I come home on Easter Sunday to find a mouse killed
as if by a surgeon. The puncture wound is a clean crescent.

I want very badly for this to mean something. I pick up
the mouse and am surprised by the fine coat with its quiet
luster like brown sugar. Briefly I resent my Siamese

with her cherubic face, the misleading glitter of her eyes.
You remind me that this is just what cats do, and this
reminder is necessary because until recent years, I knew

nothing about them nor did I care to. I did not want them
hogging my bed, shedding. Barging into poems unprompted
demanding everyone's focus. It leaves me on edge like after

that Monday fight, I heard the twist of your key and braced myself
for another round only to find you cradling a loaf of sourdough
telling me   good morning, thought you might be hungry.

I wish I could pick only the kind gestures I want but love is not about
curation so I am left with a tiny mouse in a jar, too recently cursed
with life to cremate. Briefly, I consider mummification but decide

that it isn't worth the linen. I contemplated this once before
when I found a stowaway lizard nearly invisible on the carpet
but wreathed in a drop of blood. That same moon-shaped cut

at its throat. None of this means anything, so I have found
myself once again incapable of knowing a threat from a gift.

Elegy Ending on the Pavement

The first time I saw a needle, it was
placed innocently on a nightstand as if it
was a tube of chapstick. I had no right to
see it in the bedroom of a friend's older
brother—the one who shoved me to sit
two-deep on the padded seat, then called me
a bitch when I protested. I willed him to look
at me, but his eyes steadied on the river ahead.
I craned my neck to listen to Blue Oyster Cult
tracks filtering through his headphones. Our vice
principal made him apologize, but I could tell he
wasn't sorry. Even so, his eyes when he spoke
were expectant. Lashed thickly and wide. He
smelled the same way he did on the bus: weed
and spearmint gum and clean and I wonder if this
is how he looked when he shot up. Or maybe
his eyes went moony and flat? Perhaps they were
half-closed as he spaced out to old school metal.
Even though I willed it a thousand times I can't
bear to think of those eyes in death. That earthy
faceted green was meant to shine like two ponds
spared from ripples, holy in the Appalachian sun.

Aubade for a Sister Witch in May

It's Beltane today, Carla. Your yard is how
I picture Ireland: deep green lined in green.

Are you are sleepy from traipsing after the wet
bluebells and pearls of grape hyacinth? In these

greening days, Athena comes outside with you
to study moss; she enjoys how it sponges her

paws. Athena mistakes the flowers for a bauble
toy and bats at them gently in the sun. You

scoop her up and walk into the old brick house
where your mother is playing Chopin. In houses

with perfect acoustics, every sentence uttered
aloud becomes a spell or a vow or a pledge,

this time for those newly split rubies: the bleeding
hearts who bear witness and listen. Everyone fawns

over O'Keeffe's irises and shy poppies, but I
like her bleeding hearts best which were never

afforded the shelter of a demure fold. No peekaboo
clitoris cupped and hidden. These blooms spread

out flat and look like all the most delicious parts
of the body: lungs breasts tongues every sex.

What I love most is how they grow, six ladies
in a lockstep line. The stem curves erotically

with the weight of the blossoms. Even their
color is singular. Somewhere between lipstick

and a recent wound. Perfect against all the green
of Beltane. You didn't plant them; I would say

they came to you in recognition, Carla. You are
like the bleeding heart. Not weeping, just poised

and resilient; another beauty sure to show her
best face once the Pennsylvania spring rain ends.

While Propagating Houseplants, I Find Queer Liberation

Séamus instructs me to take a curl of philodendron
and place it in water: it will
grow and keep growing   they say, waterfalling

one hand   just which way the leaves will fall.
I trust them because I've watched my mom summon
pothos   violets   palms   and lemon balm from

silt without so much as glancing at a book. I hope
I leeched this trait from her because queers like Séamus
and me have been known to soothe and nurture broken

things until their razor remnants   recognize our touch
and sigh with the labor of becoming then stretch in the joy
of indirect sunlight which I love. The window is home

to a parade a pantheon a promenade of orchids all with regal
names and dollish faces. Six months later I have sills lined
in plush green and sharp chartreuse. I steal clippings from

terracotta pots on brownstone stairs nearby. I teach them
to drink. First from a shot glass and then from a mason jar.
They are at home in Brooklyn. I prune my ginseng bonsai

to coax from it a softer shape and with each cut comes
a droplet of cream and I remember the Benjamin ficus
tree in my parents' balcony that is probably as old as I am

and how once in a while, something would compel me
to break off the tip from one pointed leaf to see the pearly
sap gush forward. How I would run my finger along this

milky edge wanting to go on lovingly breaking things to
build them up so tall that they deliver us from storms, a virus,
or radiation. I know my way around a beanstalk, but that climb

will have to wait and leave it to the law to impede upon our joy.
Look it up: this propagation is illegal as is growing anything
by any way other than seeds. Something about plant patents

as if plants came to be because a man in a white coat with
a test tube told them they could. Somewhere in here is a joke
about babymaking and men and who needs them, but leave it

to Séamus to do it their own way and build a greenhouse
in microcosm because what is a greenhouse   really
besides   light   and wet   and what is queer liberation

besides light and wet—our greatest weapons—because
we were the buried seeds that drank and wept and waited
for the day when we finally burst through concrete: a host

of golden gays for thrills and peace and war and action, the most
importance of which is tenderness which is Séamus at the window
administering fluids and medicine to those queenly blooms just
as head-turning and dazzlingly strange in this world as we are.

Is It Even A Diaspora Poem Without The Immigrant Parents' Story?
after Grace Q. Song

Make sure they were poor and even if not,
make sure they were poor at some point.
This especially important if you are Brahmin:
no one wants to hear about the white people
who aren't kind to you in the airport. You're
in the fucking airport. Do you hear yourself?
If your parents love each other, say that. If
your parents do not love each other, lie. If
your parents were in an arranged marriage,
you'll need a good vignette about them bonding
over Blade Runner in theaters, blasting Foreigner
on the radio on the way to the bank in the sedan given
to them by kindly neighbors. White people in the 80s were
cool, maybe because you could still buy quaaludes
and the coke was wicked. Make sure at least one of your
parents has a charming talent or hobby like sewing or
violin. Don't make them athletes in the pool, bankers,
chefs, or soldiers. Nothing too aggressive or ambitious.
Erase the part where your mother gives up her
career to care for the children; say she only wanted
to be a mom. Don't mention her Olympic-caliber track
records, and omit the botched knee surgery. No worries
if your parents didn't party or do any cool drugs;
Americans like their immigrants squeaky clean.
Leave out the part about your mom throwing
up on New Year's Eve, how your dad opens the door
and places her limp in the shower as there was nowhere
else to sit in the studio apartment. If you had a violent
childhood, remove the kitchen utensils from all the fights
but one. Be sure to mention the war, any war. Just as long
as there's war. At your book signing, white people
will ask you if your parents are proud. You'll loudly
say something like HA HA, IN THEIR OWN WAY,
YEAH! Your cover needs no less than three of the

following: paisley, peacock feathers, Ganesha,
gold leaf, Buddha, an oil lamp, incense, the ocean,
and/or your mother and father, waving goodbye.

The Trouble Is

that I was in a 4th of July parade when I was three or four
in a red wagon on loan from Cassie who decorated
and pulled the spangled thing, a sparkler in her other hand.
The parade was marvelous, tambourines and honking
horns and white teeth like Cassie's. I did my duty. I smiled
and waved my flag, bound to the wagon like I am
bound to the nation, bound to Cassie and 200 more beautiful
white girls with strawberry braids, denim overalls, & perfect
constellations of freckles. The trouble is that first I learned
to read, then I learned patriotism, then I learned to walk.
America lives inside me, a hungry beauty who will never love
me back, and I say I hate America, but I can't imagine life
without the scent of honey-roasted nuts in Union Square
or the petrichor of the Susquehanna River Valley when the moss
swells under the black walnut trees. The trouble is that I love
Tennessee whiskey and Kentucky bourbon as much as I love
Viognier and scotch. I love brash vendors, red bagged chips,
& the Cajun cry of HEY, BABY! when I order a shrimp po'boy.
I love wild mushrooms & corn & clean wheat & rich cheese,
Firm and proud in her wheel. There's nothing like Wisconsin
extra sharp cheddar, the only cheese meant to marry macaroni.
Don't test me on this, I will fight anyone who disagrees.
America makes you do this, makes you get violent over noodles.
The trouble is that I hate America, but I love gas stations, apple-
picking, & Bloomsburg pumpkin vendors who leave wares on
the roadside with an empty coffee can for the cash. Even today,
they still trust the honor system, because American love is as
ferocious as American hate. America's heart is wreathed in
flames, swear words, & tricolor popsicles that drip down to
your elbow in a sticky smear. See the trouble is that I hate America,
but she hated me first, and despite white boys with their guns
and televangelicals in their gaudy megachurches, there are still
so many anchors tethered to my flesh, weighing me down,
binding me to this wicked, dazzling place, to the red wagon,
to the eternal question of Oh say, can you see?
to the promise of freedom and a full belly, whatever the cost.

ACKNOWLEDGEMENTS

Love and gratitude to the following publications where versions of these poems first appeared:

ANMLY. "Men."

Anti-Heroin Chic. "Crystal Fisticuffs for Messy Mystics Who Like Rings."

Appalachian Review. "Half Ode to the Rope Swing I Never Climbed" and "A Snake Heart Can Slide Up and Down the Length of Its Body."

Bayou Magazine. "I Cancel Your Plane Tickets."

Bluebottle Review. "To Protect Your Children, You Need a Drawer of Hair and Teeth."

The Boiler. "Elegy in August Town."

CALYX. "Ode to Bathroom Mirror Altars I've Built for Myself" and "While Propagating Houseplants, I Find Queer Liberation."

Copper Nickel. "On Having a Loud Ass Mouth."

Frontier Poetry. "Elegy for Fakir Musafar, the Father of Modern Body Piercing."

Heavy Feather Review. "In Hell, I Study Busking, Smut, and Stares" and "Litany of Bad Habits, Millennial Edition."

Hooligan Magazine. "Abecedarian for a Sale on Cremation" and "On Dumb Souvenirs and the Taking Spirit."

Jet Fuel Review. "Don't Trifle With Baboon Queens" and "Kyrielle with the Crown Jewels."

The Journal. "Self-Portrait as Samus Aran, 1986."

Kissing Dynamite. "Magnolia Striptease."

Kweli Journal. "Banana Heart."

New Orleans Review. "Is It Even A Diaspora Poem Without the Immigrant Parents' Story?"

The Offing. "Voicemail for Emily Dickinson."

Poetry Is Currency. "Self-Portrait as the Birthing Statue in Men (2022)" and "While Cooking Salmon Sous Vide, I Consider the Futility of Courtship."

Passages North. "The Trouble Is."

Poet Lore. "Aubade for a Sister Witch in May."

Pussy Magic. "Pink Ladies' Smoke Session."

Rubbertop Review. "Nocturne with Helium Balloons Lost on the Denver Airport Ceiling."

Salamander Magazine. "Self-Portrait as Saint Rita of Cascia Covered in Bees, 1381."

Sierra Nevada Review. "All Nests Begin in the Body."

Sonora Review. "Elegy Ending on the Pavement" and "Elegy With Threats, Gifts, and Dead Mice."

The Worcester Review. "Love Song for the First Dyke Bartender."

About RITA MOOKERJEE

RITA MOOKERJEE is an assistant professor of Interdisciplinary Studies at Worcester State University. Her research has been funded by the Fulbright Foundation and the National Endowment for the Humanities. She is the author of *False Offering* (JackLeg Press). Her poems can be found in *CALYX, Copper Nickel, New Orleans Review, the Offing,* and *Poet Lore.* She serves as an editor at *Split Lip Magazine, Sundress Publications,* and *Honey Literary.*

www.ingramcontent.com/pod-product-compliance
Lightning Source LLC
Chambersburg PA
CBHW020218090426
42734CB00008B/1124